FOREST BOOKS

EYES FROM A DREAM

AGNETA PLEIJEL was born 1940, in Stockholm. After taking her MA in 1973 she worked variously as a journalist, editor, translator and academic. Since 1987 she has been President of Swedish PEN. After turning freelance in 1981 she began to write. Her first two books were collections of poems, of which *Eyes from a Dream* is the second. She had already written several plays, for stage, film and media. Her first novel, *Vindspejare* (He who Observeth the Wind, 1987), has won several Swedish awards. Her second, *Hundstjärnan* (Dog Star), is the story of a young girl. 'He Who Observeth the Wind' is partly autobiographical, following a journey Agneta and her mother made to Indonesia in Agneta's grandfather's footsteps. He went to Dutch East India in 1894 and married an Indonesian girl. The novel describes this artist *manqué* and his confrontation with the exotic land where he lived for 30 years, and to which Agneta felt herself drawn. But in 1981 she went on a cultural journey to Poland, and the sufferings of the people there inspired many of the poems in *Eyes from a Dream*. She married her Polish husband after this trip. The poems express the strange dichotomy of agony and caring love in this century.

ANNE BORN is a poet, translator and historian. Her last translation for Forest Books was *Spring Tide*, a selection of poems by the Danish poet Pia Tafdrup. She has also translated for Forest, *Snow and Summers* by Solveig von Schoultz and *Room Without Walls* by Bo Carpelan.

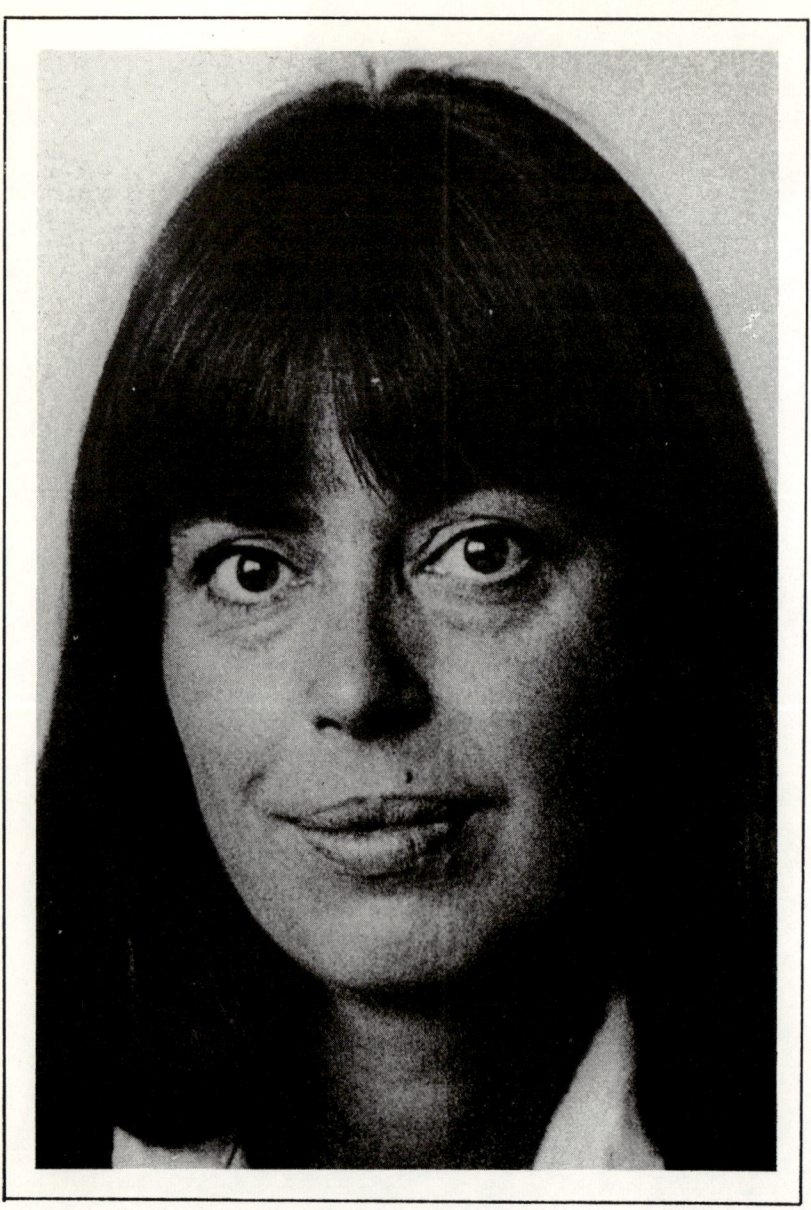

Agneta Pleijel

Eyes from a Dream

Poems by

Agneta Pleijel

FOREST
BOOKS
London & Boston

Translated from the Swedish by Anne Born

PUBLISHED BY
FOREST BOOKS

20 Forest View, Chingford, London E4 7AY, U.K.
61 Lincoln Road, Wayland, MA 01778, U.S.A.

FIRST PUBLISHED 1991

Typeset in Great Britain by Cover to Cover, Cambridge
Printed in Great Britain by BPCC Wheatons Ltd, Exeter

ISBN 1 85610 015 4

*A catalogue record for this book
is available from the British Library*

Library of Congress Catalogue Card No.:

91–72164

Forest Books gratefully acknowledge the support of
the Swedish Institute and the financial support of the
Arts Council of Great Britain

The original publication, *Ögon ur en Dröm*,
was published by Norstedts Forlag, Stockholm

Contents

Introduction

I don't know any more what I should do
about streets and houses, old people and cathedrals
or films that sigh with history and memories
I feel helpless and sorrowful

This is the fifth stanza of Agneta Pleijel's powerful, long (16 stanzas and final line of coda) poem: 'The sound of schoolchildren at play'. Although it has been placed late in the book, that sound dominates the volume. The tone is plangent, memorialising. Words and lines barb themselves into the reader's mind like 'Voices . . . calling . . . out of the shadows':

Always this insistent presence of what is past
I cannot give shelter to what has meant most to me
We're found nowhere but in what is scattered
How fearful sorrow is when it stays out of reach

These Rilkean lines chosen from different stanzas almost make another, the essence of this extraordinary poem.

Agneta Pleijel has written in various forms – novels and plays as well as two other books of poems. The project of all her work seems to be the retrieval of the past; not only her own personal past, but that of her country and the countries she is connected to by ties of blood and marriage: Sweden, Java, and Poland.

Her first novel, *Vindspejare* (He Who Observeth the Wind), is a complex first-person narrative combining the responses of a mature and thoughtful woman with a sensuous intensity of childhood recollection and the story of her grandfather. He spent 30 years in Indonesia, then returned with a Javanese wife to a house in the south of Sweden where he planted fruit orchards and constructed strange stone monuments and edifices like petrified poems. Much later, Agneta Pleijel accompanied her 70-year-old mother on the long-planned return journey to the very house where she had grown up in Surabaya. Perhaps this experience was one of the triggers for the novel.

Agneta Pleijel was already a well-known literary figure in Sweden when the novel was published in 1987. As well as her poetry, several of her plays had been successfully produced, and she has been a journalist, editor, translator and academic. Two years later, in 1989, the novel *Hundstjärnan* (Dog Star) appeared. I remember the impact Stig Dagerman's stories had on me when I read them in the early 1950s. This book shares that quality – the power to create an image as rich and dense and mysterious as an ikon, every line and colour chosen to emphasise its emotional and spiritual meaning.

The same power is evident in the poetry. In the four-part poem that opens this collection, 'Polonaise in A major, opus 30 no 1', a troubling and profound moral consciousness is enclosed within the framework of description and response to a piece of music which the poet's mother is teaching schoolgirls to play on the piano during the Second World War. The first lines are:

A grey winter afternoon, faint piano music
Suddenly I stand at memory's half-open door
and weep: I can hardly read yet
but I know already there's a kind of music
that can drown us

and the final stanza evokes the worst aspects of that and every other war and yet somehow includes the possibility of hope:

Now I hear despair play in my mother
And while she plays a world is shattered out there
Those already crushed come swimming up
In their mouth every one of them holds
a fragment of an extinguished star

Two long sequences, 'Polish Suit I' and 'Polish Suite II', dated respectively May and December 1981, extend the range in space as well as time. These poems express a decent reticence and sense of insufficiency in the face of that country's tragic history. The first poem of 'Suite I' concludes: 'I have no memories, all is memory here.' The metaphor of a painful and doubtful birth recurs, as does the hope of such renewal.

The last section is titled 'A Winter in Stockholm', and includes 'The sound of schoolchildren at play'. As in the Polish Suites, there are several prose poems. This form has been used by Tomas Tranströmer and other Scandinavian poets, perhaps more often and effectively than happens in England, and the five prose poems that begin this sequence are fine examples: compressed and yet specific, profound yet not portentous. It is as though a camera zoomed forward onto miscroscopic detail then backwards for a total panoramic view.

Eyes from a Dream is Agneta Pleijel's first volume of poems to be translated and published in England. The translations are most successful – by which I mean that they read like poems written in English, and Anne Born is to be congratulated. This strong profound voice from the north must surely be attended to with admiration and pleasure.

Ruth Fainlight
1991

We do not understand the nature of fidelity if we fail to realise that fidelity is an essential constituent of hope. Hope points us towards some kind of future; through hope the future holds value for us.

From *The Ethics of Solidarity*
by Jozef Tischner

I

Polonaise in A major, opus 40 no 1

Polonaise in A Major

1

En vintereftermiddags gråljus, avlägsen pianomusik
Plötsligt står jag vid minnets halvöppna dörr
och gråter: jag kan väl knappast ännu läsa
men vet redan att det finns en musik
som kan dränka oss

Låg himmel, noppiga tapeter, fyrtiotal
Vid pianot mamma med tillbakakastat huvud
Hon mjukar upp fingrarna som inför den stora konserten
Den stora musiken spelar i min mamma
Och nu lyfter hon sina händer

Nu spelar hon Frédéric Chopin, en polonäs
I tamburens mörker trampar stora flickor
med shinglat hår och obekanta drömmar
Hur kan man pressa hängivelse
ur så magra kroppar? Min mamma spelar

Polonaise in A Major

1

A grey winter afternoon, faint piano music
Suddenly I stand at memory's half open door
and weep: I can hardly read yet
but I know already there's a kind of music
that can drown us

Lowering skies, flock wallpaper, the forties
Mamma at the piano with head thrown back
softens up her fingers as if before a concert
Great music plays within my mother
And now she lifts her hands

She's playing Frederic Chopin, a polonaise
Big girls shuffle out in the dark hall
with shingled hair and strange wild dreams
How can you squeeze commitment
from such thin bodies? My mother plays

2

She's the piano teacher, it's war and winter
Out of despair you become monk or soldier
Or neither, just slowly go to pieces
Now the last bars of Chopin die away
Liberty bleeds to death in an A major chord

There is a longing that's without a name
My mother tugs hard at her pupil's woollen jacket
each time the skinny girlish hands stumble
and go wrong   There is a longing that can crush us
My mother builds it into an étude by Czerny-Krentzlin

There is a land of darkness, of love without limit
A resignation that demands each breath
There is a final leap towards the abyss
You can ponder a thousand times but only once
make a decision or go under

3

Or choose the leap and go under
There's an ocean there within my mother
that lacks outlet and name and can drown us
A tug at the woollen sleeve: the girl's fingers run
an obedient race on the piano's school sports ground

I stand in the door, can barely read
but already know I belong to this inland sea
Already know this music plays in us
The girl's fingers run as on glassy ice
And my mother holds her hand still

There is a music that can really drown us
if we don't lock it up behind bars:
bar-lines, pause sign, key and repeat
All music wants to escape from these signs
that hold us and it in captivity

4

My mother plays, it is evening and winter
Herr Hitler speaks from Berlin out of our Concerton,
the green eye sucks Papa's silent shadow into itself
Mamma plays Herr Chopin, a polonaise
Suffering is all and it can drown us

and the world. This evening Mamma plays
as if she wants to shatter the piano
It must be shattered. The world must be shattered
In the end the sea must find the river
that leads the water to a greater sea

Now I hear despair play in my mother
And while she plays a world is shattered out there
Those already crushed come swimming up
In their mouth every one of them holds
a fragment of an extinguished star

II

Polish suite I
(May 1981)

The city

A rooster wakes me each morning
    outside the tower block window
When I lean out
    I see a peasant leading his cow
And further off petrol fumes

The history of Poland drops
    swiftly through the hour glass
Someone turns it, everything starts afresh
    I travel through glass
All's as real as the living eye

At the national museum Rejtan still lies
    in a painting by Matejko
tearing at his breast
    He wants to give warning of traitors
And they're already gathering in the doorway

Dandelion seeds snow over Warsaw,
    cover Penderecki where he sits
in the park, frozen into marble
    On the steps of the Palace of Culture
pigeons mess about as they did in a prewar time

Dandelion seeds snow over the city,
    cover the ghetto stones, cover
memory, the kisses and sorrow
    Fragments of history still lie
undiscovered under the stones

All this hope of homecoming
    Dead friends, ancestors' dead bones
Trees, blowing with promises
    in the Lazienki park
I have no memories, all is memory here

Train journey

On the train between Warsaw and Gdansk
    I doze off and dream
I'm travelling along a narrow river
    deeper and deeper into the dark lands

On a dark river in a flat bottomed boat
    through a landscape where bones rest close
like torches in a parade of demonstrators
    under the scorched black earth

The blind make way for each other
    Children scream inaudibly like bats
The darkness is soft as cotton

Death lurks so close under each face
    Life so close under each death
Here live the dead and the unborn

Here lives the sun the dark woman
    each night before she sets light to day
Someone touches my arm, the oarsman

He whispers that no one ever arrives
    Love is a river of darkness
It flows through the land of the dead and unborn
    It's never ending, you never arrive

Wake with the sun squeaking
    its brakes outside the train window
Someone gives me a piece
    of strongly scented orange

The lung

Here in these streets, in these cities
    where human faces have only just been washed clean,
actions and handshakes washed too
    something inevitable is happening

Which maybe happens only in the cracks
    between one phase and the next
that cement our history together
    and later on are so hard to discern

    With no special effort the sun seems
to have stopped itself in its tracks, stands still
    over Cracow's Stary Rynek

2

On the cool stone floor in Czestochova
    a woman lies with her forehead against the stone
In the murmuring human throng of the cathedral
    she's spread out her arms to make a cross

Like a great ship that in deathly silence
    slips from the dock into the water
and just waits for wind to lift her!
    A human deliverance is under way

    The bodies around me are worn
But within them pulse human beings
    waiting to be born

3

As if all was one great breathing
    As if the epochs of civilisations
could be described as one great breathing
    As if we all pulsed in the same great body

As if human beings were spinning
    in the huge lung whose breath
took them ever nearer delivery
    And then again further away

    And as if in that moment
we were very close, and the lung's foetal membrane
    close to breaking point

The painter

The flat is dark and her neck
very white, eyes full of fear
We live here like rats
in our dark holes
and once again
I've packed my bag,
she says

Her husband went away
years ago to the USA
a successful sculptor and professor
She shows some pictures
I prefer to live
where I feel at home,
she says

I paint and smoke
The fool's naked face, taken
from a painting by Matejko,
glimmers on a canvas: art's
strength and powerlessness
confronting power,
she says

It's raining in Warsaw, Solidarnosc
stubbornly and step by step
achieves the impossible
The most fearful
are those who dare not believe
Where there's no fear
there's no widsom

Movements

1

This is the morning before everything. Sunlight
floats through my room like icefloes. Everything is
possible. Everything is stacked together: hunger,
salt, blood. Something is on the way. I know what it
is: everything I've avoided, everything I've put off.
Terror walks in me with stone shoes. Outside the
window the piles of the foreign city have been
driven into the fields. It looks like a photograph. It
is real as stones. In a moment it could collapse.
(We must dare to believe. Otherwise everything
is really lost.)

2

The foreign troops are ranged along the border. The soldiers' faces are young and untouched. Power flows through their veins. At a distance or in photographs you can make out their faces like patches of darkness. For a long time a different kind of darkness has lived within me, I call it hopelessness. You put your arm around my waist. The horse chestnuts have burst out into white laughter. The city stretches itself, breathes. A smile is reflected in the river, the grass, in your eyes, in the colourful umbrellas in the square. It is still hesitant, as if it expected something.

3

We walk along a narrow ray of light, surrounded by darkness. Hope has been alive in me all this winter. Your body has breathed close to mine. I cannot separate you from the child. The child lives within us. For so many years I have pushed hope aside, lived in brief paragraphs, fumbled for green, dared not believe it would be born from the bare branch. You go away from me, but I can't grasp your absence. You are here. We walk through the city in sunlight.

4

Light rainfall this morning early. I recognised the scent of it from some early summer morning in my childhood. The rain has stopped but the scent lingers. Now the ray of light has widened into a sea. The little human boats have launched out. They have waited so long. Now they hoist sail. One by one they leave the shore and make for the open sea. We know already: they have called a strike along the whole of the north coast. The telephone lines have been cut. There's no longer any turning back.

5

A little while ago there was stone here. Now the image of a human being is growing out of the stone. The face rests in itself as in a carving by an African sculptor from Ife. It is calm and still, open like a steppe landscape. The eyes and hands are open. This person resembles a child who has seen everything and is without fear. Soon she will release herself from the stone. Her skin will be human skin. No sculptor will strike her out of the stone. She rises from it herself and it crumbles away behind her. A whole nation rises from the stone.

6

Dread nails me down. Its iron cramps go right through my body. I cannot breathe. My face falls in splinters down into my cupped hands. I put down the newspaper, the strange language flickers behind my eyelids. It speaks of trust, what is written between the lines? Violence sharpens its spear. All is ready. You and I cannot give each other a child. The soldiers stand at the frontiers to east, south, west. Their faces are stone. When the light falls on them they crack and make way for identical stone faces.

7

But nothing is yet decided. There is a needle's eye. The city is bathed in light. We walk through the streets together, over the bridges, down towards the river. Your body is so close to mine. The outcome is not given in advance although the knives are held to the throat. A whole nation rises out of the stone, willingly approaches the knives. Down by the river the light is painfully strong like a great joy. Children play at the water's edge. The people rise out of the stone.

III

Polish suite II
(December 1981)

Ögon ur en dröm

1

Drömmer att någon avkläder mig huden
Det är i Warszawa men i drömmen går jag
i ett nordiskt hus, timrat, en fäbod
där jag aldrig varit men dit jag ofta återvänt

Och så, hudlös, och i stor smärta
möter jag honom som jag har förrått
Han stiger fram i ljusdunklet, en vanställd
Skelettet har halvt rasat samman
av att jag vågat tro så litet

Men när han lyfter sin blick
är den mild som en blomma, en susning
Och det är allt

Eyes from a dream

Dream someone's taking off my skin
It's in Warsaw but in the dream I'm in
a Nordic house, timbered, a shieling
where I've never been but often gone back to

And then, raw and in great pain
I meet the one I betrayed
He comes out of the dim light, deformed
His skeleton has half caved in
because I had so little trust

But when he lifts his eyes
they are gentle as flowers, a soughing
And that is all

2

And as if the dream was a foreboding
that what has happened will happen a thousand times
when I wake I remember
that recently I met those eyes I dreamed of

In a backstreet cathedral with its whispering coolness
its votive tablets, its mumbling song
I met the eyes of he who in Auschwitz
gave his life so that another might live:
Kolbe, with gentle eyes

An amateur likeness, hastily drawn
Prison clothes, short trousers, crooked body
And those eyes

3

Now the secret police and the riot squad
gather in the cafés of Warsaw
They say the error of calculation is corrected
And the gap in the armature filled.

They say the prison windows are already covered
by the floating leaves of Lazienki park
I can hear the echo of axe blows myself
from those who long since gave up
I sit among the traitors and hear axe blows

I am without a skin
and don't know where I belong
I who had so little trust

4

There's everything here in this overcivilised violence
The mass graves too with their riches
And the printing presses with their maimed fingers
And the whisperings among the living

And the silent wanderings in squares and streets
while the radio sends out its bulletins
And the hundreds of candle ends in windows
when they form a huge cross
against the evening's dark house bodies

And the gentle eyes from the dream
that whisper death too
lives for the future's sake

To an involuntary emigrant

How you felt something creep closer
Closer to the city, to the skin
and to the blood,
this secret transport system

Now there's no turning back
And you must tell the truth or almost the truth
or lie at an office in the Bronx
or in Paris or Stockholm

Of course there are movements back there
Words on thin or torn paper reach you
That's what it's like for them back there
But you happened to find yourself outside

The future's put forward again
The leaven mixed with three measures of flour
permeated much but not everything
No, not enough

You smoke cigarettes and propagate
an ever obscurer message
Before, all was real as paving stones
And long prepared

And you tell yourself the mustard seed isn't dead
but waits for water
But some you also remember
carried hopelessness inside them a long time
like a stone heart

And the rulers and the newsreaders
in this new land have no need of your truth
No, not of the whole of your truth
Hardly even a fraction of your truth
It's too simple

Man's tireless work
His movements in dance or memory
his glance of green waters, blue acres

And this floating smell of dung
And this written out demand remain

13.12.1981

A letter

So she returns to the underground
The newspapers, pamphlets, journeyings
        as during the war. And after the war
And now again this war

Her description is circulated, features
nailed fast to the screen. One afternoon
        she's offered a lift in an army car
Gives her own address by mistake

And is politely taken home
Safe back she opens her fridge door
        where two terrified carrier pigeons throb
She kisses their eyes and beaks

And sends them out into the world:
        I'm alive! We're still alive

A poet

Stanislav Ignacy Witkiewicz
goes out into Warsaw's streets one morning early
to buy bread and candles
In this hour of the police a shabby dame
on her way to work meets him
Asks: What brings Mister Poet out
at such a raw hour of dawning?
Answers Witkacy: Noble lady, it's long
since I lived among the living
Therefore I can walk these streets
without discomfort, without pleasure

The frozen map

1

Where we once journeyed together it's frozen
On the ice perhaps still a film of living tears
But the country has frozen again into its map image
where all is surveyed, regulated, registered

Military bases, missiles, dreams,
swiftly written love letters, telephone calls
The dogs bark at night as usual
Those homeless flocks that with their measured freedom
measure time: when they fall silent it's morning

Across this map we once moved together
in the car's small loophole of darkness,
maps spread out on our knees, thermos and sandwiches
And we stayed without leave with sensible women
who had seen much, and the lilacs were in bloom

Holy Mother of God, and grass still grows there
and where we once drove off the road by mistake
Europe still smells of farmyard dung

2

You said: only he
who holds a memory of summer
deep in himself really freezes
I answered: say if the dream of summer
is only a trick
to make those who're freezing
endure the cold?
And who, you asked, can meddle
with our innermost dream
like that?
I had no answer
Won't allow power a greater power
than it has

3

There's a story:
How by fires and in the barracks,
in camps and in the endless wilds of exile,
they suddenly felt a presence, sharp as a lightray
A moment of tremendous joy
And knew then
that another time
would come

4

There's a story:
How deep inside the mammoth's body
they found a foetus, fully formed (and perfect)
Like a huge memory the ice had preserved
this infant

IV

A winter in Stockholm

From my window

1

How this city floats directly over the horizon on a
winter afternoon outside my window. How a black
air balloon rises straight up into the middle of the
sky over there near Högalid. How all colours are
painfully clear, how all yeses and nos balance each
other until there's nothing to say. How the bare
trees hold their breath in inexpressible pain. And
then the sky breaks as if with a shriek: life's order
is unacceptable, madness lies close beneath the
treacherous surface of existence, the barbed wire
flowers sprouting out of the earth cut into the flesh

2

And just outside the eye's field of vision another city: childhood's. Trees lean their heads over the cradle, whisper, sigh, sing secrets, ask questions: which of us does this child resemble, the maple or the quivering aspen? The linden with its heavy perfume, the petrified oak? These trees have such dark eyes. They sigh, they bend their crowns close together above the child, they are happy. And the child already resembles a little tree, it soughs in all its limbs. Already the eye mirrors the whole sea, the whole sky

3

And between these two points: a beach. Who built
it, who sprinkled grains of sand, threw out blocks
of stone, organised the imprint of our naked
bodies in the sand? It must be a long time since
anyone lay here in the sun with their newspaper.
With the telescope we try to catch up with memory
when it removes itself to the far side of the year's
crest. The gull is fixed to the flaking gold knob on
top of the flagstaff. On the satellite picture the
tanks are planted all along the borderline, even the
pitched tents are discernible

4

Everything is simultaneous. Even that which has been and that which approaches. It is only the movement itself that's lost. Blood drips slowly from the mouth of the green pump. It always leaked, why did no one mend it. Deep down in the stones under the bathing hut pier is my father's lost gold watch. Last year's reeds rustle like eggshells. Our breaths blow like lost winds through the scattered treetops. Someone has counted them. Someone always counts them. There's always one too many. Who among us has breathed in this crazy enterprise to deprive order of its tribute?

To the unborn

Can those who have never been born grieve? Can they weep, who have never been allowed to live? A strange thought, but how otherwise can I sense this breathing just outside my window? From where otherwise do these cries come, these soft and importunate voices? I have to believe they exist and that they grieve. Today darkness is no protection and the light no solace. The city floats away in the fog, how strangely demanding it is. Now I'm in panic-stricken flight and nothing comes closer to me. I hear the shrill voices of the dead, they scare me, and I have nothing to offer. My own imprisonment is also theirs. Outside the window I glimpse the contours of everything that wanted to be but never became: tree, root system, colours

The sound of schoolchildren at play

Voices are always calling even out of the shadows
The sound of schoolchildren at play is very clear,
awakes disquiet, a sough of sorrow, the taste of injustice
Does all freedom taste like this while it is with us?

Images rise before me of snorting horses
Cavalry, flags of honour, vassals' proud fidelity
And the king flying over it all, a benevolent
smiling cloud, soon covering the whole landscape . . .

All this is shadowy but clear, has existed, lies
before us like an amazing heap of ruins, doesn't exist
Always this insistent presence of what's past
And every day I wade in oblivion

My sisters and I walked hand in hand up a hill
and whispering came from the bones of the dead
or my mother's mysterious sorrow. I don't know yet
I cannot give shelter to what has meant most to me

I don't know any more what I should do
about streets and houses, old people and cathedrals
or films that sigh with history and memories
I feel helpless and sorrowful

My sister's body against mine on a glass verandah
She wanted Mamma and cried, I loathed her
The air was motionless on that verandah
I still get the taste of honeysuckle, forbidden things,
                                        dead wasps

I don't know how to speak about all this,
it is so irrevocably gone, and yet exists
And this photograph of my youngest sister at some
                                        dining table
She turns her head away, swallowing revolt

as if something had already died in her, but when?
How all is scattered: hope, wild shame,
windblown leaves, water, pictures of us
We're found nowhere but in what is scattered

How does History taste? Before me a rose in a vase
is dying with a terribly human gesture
For three days I've watched its course but cannot see
when it irrevocably happens

But I see my mother's body, overcome
As when a solitary woman walks over the battlefield
amazed it is possible to bring about so much death
And she does not find the one she seeks, he is gone

Something irrevocable has happened, it's bewildering
Sorrow is hurled like a cannonball over the sky, fixed
like a pomegranate that glimmers on the branch
nearest the sun, elusive, out of reach

How fearful sorrow is when it stays out of reach
It leaves dearth and emptiness, we all wander
in such dearth, when did it happen? I don't know
But I feel we grow less and less visible

In museums I tend to look for historical paintings
I love emblems and kingly glances, pictures
of hounds and horses, of heralds and cupbearers and of
strange meetings between enemies beneath lofty tents

Look, how they build staircases for each other to climb
I love this haughty ruler waiting up there,
his resolute features, right foot striding on,
in short, this proclaimed summing-up of time

One summer evening I saw my father for the first time
He stood on a wooden bridge surrounded by black water
He wept. He pushed his fingers through his hair. Said:
Think of it, to reach 40 without knowing who you are

Then he and the bridge floated away on the black water
What had happened? Who can tell
what's happened to us now living. Something once alive
stays on in our blood like a whisper:

unease, the sough of sorrow, a taste of injustice

It feels like an absence

It feels like an absence
I can't find a better word
It feels as if I'm only a fraction
or less than present here where I am
The face in the mirror is absent
And skin and cells: absent

Each evening I have to undress myself of restlessness
just as you take off your own muscles
I drown in the white ceiling above me
But it's hard to answer the telephone any more
or write those urgent letters
or even put some sort of order
into the mass of papers on my table

Hear far below the rush of cars out there
the quiet murmur like a Jurassic river
as it flows towards some kind of primeval sea
Barely audible, painfully audible
I have to listen, and the restlessness grows

Things outdistance me with their voices,
so maddeningly insistent with assurances of their presence
and saying they will all survive me
because they're still going with the stream

But below the traffic noise this other sound:
the quiet pattering of a flock of goats
on their way up a primevally ancient cliff
that no longer exists

Weight

Who has put this weight in me
The weight of a rose that does not wither

The weight of an egg that doesn't fall
The weight of a hammer that doesn't strike

God, let me wake one morning to your
lightness, go out whistling into your light

The dead queen

There is a queen who rules
over the kingdom of death
By her magic arts she turns blood into ice
and ice into stone
She rides on her black horse
restlessly from frontier to frontier
In her stone tower
she holds a young man prisoner
Every spring a shudder goes
through the dead queen
Then she remembers the time
he succeeded in getting into her kingdom

He came from one of the neighbouring
vassal countries
That year there was a severe drought
in the lands of the living
He was commissioned to capture the queen
and carry her across the border
Then her frozen tears would melt
and flood over the dry earth

It's said he arrived at evening

He made his way past her dead sentries
The stone gate was higher than he had expected
but he was armed with his innocence
He knocked three times
and the fourth time he was let in
The doors seemed to open in haste

First he met her glassy gaze
He opened it with his gaze of light
He met her mouth of ice
with his living kiss
Her embrace was a vault of iron
He opened it with his burning fire
That's how it went

And that's how it is: he whose task is urgent
cannot linger on the threshold:
he must go in
And the stone gates closed behind them both

And they loved
Every night he thrust his tongue of fire
into her frozen sex
Every morning she cooled his hot brow
with her breast of stone
And her frozen tears melted
and watered the dry earth
The rivers were filled
and the waterfalls sang
and butterflies fluttered over the fields
Many children were born
in the adjacent lands
and in her kingdom

But she wanted him to stay
and he did not want that
He wanted to take her hotfoot over the border
But she did not want that
Then she imprisoned him in the tower
and had him turned to stone

Now when she went to visit him
her cold hands could get no warmth from him
He sat withdrawn into himself
listening to the stone songs
of her stone birds
Then her tears froze into ice
Then drought came again to the fields
The cold spread from her kingdom
into the neighbouring lands
Not even those who were very old
could recall such cold

Now she rides as before
from frontier to frontier

of her stony kingdom
No empire has lasted as long as hers
not even the Assyrian or the Roman
No captivity has been as petrified as his
not even the Babylonian

One cannot know the outcome
of such a meeting
before it has taken place
Not even if it takes place thousands of times
Not even if it is told in thousands of tales
Not even the statistics with their calculations . . .

Every spring a shudder goes through the queen
of the kingdom of death
It is that poets sing about,
so strong is their hope

The winter

This winter I get the feeling that the land I'm living in has been forgotten. Here or there some frozen rocks or an islet rise out of the water. Later, forgetfulness washes over the stones again. I get the feeling that someone is dreaming the land and dreaming us, so that we rise up into reality in patches. And in my own dreams this winter, inexplicable and clear, there are glimpses of people who seem to signal something inaudible and important. I imagine that I myself am a sign in their dreams, a kind of cry from a very long and very arctic winter. I realise the winter must come to an end some day. I picture to myself how then we who dreamed each other will see and touch each other

Other Scandinavian Titles
Published by Forest Books

ROOM WITHOUT WALLS

Selected poems of Bo Carpelan

Translated from the Swedish by Anne Born

Perhaps the greatest poet writing in Finland today, Bo Carpelan takes much of his inspiration from the landscape of Finland, its stern northern wintry presence and its delicate spring and summer. In style concise, pure and clear, in form economical, he writes with a delicate lyrical beauty of fundamental human experience. Beneath the spare, deceptively simple surface lie vast eternities, gentle echoes, mysteries, sorrows, signs and warnings.

ISBN 0 948259 08 6   paper £6.95   144pp illustrated

THE HOUR OF THE LYNX

A play by Per Olov Enquist

Translated by Ross Shideler

A young boy is committed to a psychiatric institution for a motiveless murder. A sensitive and challenging play, *The Hour of the Lynx* focuses on the boy's role in a controlled experiment in which the researcher gives him a cat to care for. The pastor and the researcher struggle to understand the boy's complex emotional riddles which ultimately reveal profound insights into the mystery and miracle of love and salvation. Enquist is one of Scandinavia's foremost dramatists; productions of his work in Scandinavian and European theatres have established him as a leading European writer.

ISBN 0 948259 85 X   paper £6.95   64pp

PREPARATIONS FOR FLIGHT
& OTHER SWEDISH STORIES

Translated by Robin Fulton

Robin Fulton, one of the best-known translators of contemporary Swedish literature, has gathered a collection of stories which, as he says in his preface, remained in his mind long after a first reading. In all of them, concrete reality evokes mystery, and in many of them, childhood reflections affect and are affected by everyday adult experience.

ISBN 0 9482599 66 3   paper £8.95   176pp

THE NAKED MACHINE

Poems by Matthías Johannessen

Translated by Marshall Brement

This is the first volume of a contemporary Icelandic poet to be published in English. Already translated into many languages, Matthías Johannessen is acknowledged as one of Iceland's greatest living poets. The translator, Marshall Brement, is also a poet and met Johannessen while American Ambassador to Iceland.

ISBN 0 948259 43 4   paper £5.95   96pp illustrated
ISBN 0 948259 44 2   cloth £7.95   96pp illustrated

HEARTWORK

by Solveig von Schoultz

Translated from the Swedish
by Marlaine Delargy & Joan Tate

Winner of numerous literary prizes, Solveig von
Schoultz is widely acknowledged as one of Finland's
leading poets and prose writers. 'Her short stories',
writes Bo Carpelan, 'present an acute and subtle analysis
of human relationships – between adults and children,
men and women, and between different genera-
tions . . . She is not only a listener and an observer: she
is also passionately involved with these dramas of
everyday life which are all concerned with the problems
of human value and human growth. These she portrays
without sentimentality but with the rich perception of
experience.'

ISBN 0 948259 60 7   paper £7.95   144pp

SNOW AND SUMMERS

by Solveig von Schoultz

Translated from the Swedish by Anne Born

Snow and Summers presents the cream of von Schoultz's
poetry from almost fifty years for the first time in
English. 'For both poet and reader', writes Bo Carpelan,
'von Schoultz's poetry is an exercise in the sharpening
of vision . . . sincerity and smiling wisdom engendered
by a lifetime of experience.'

ISBN 0 948259   paper £7.95   128pp

THE SEER
AND OTHER NORWEGIAN STORIES

by Jonas Lie

Translated by Brian Morton
& Richard Trevor

Trolls or unconscious impulses? Jonas Lie, Norway's great nineteenth century writer, had by his own admission, a twilight nature. Like the landscape, it shifted from light to dark in a fantastic world of superstition. *The Seer* and eight other shorter stories reveal the progress over a period of time towards that darkening vision – towards the belief that within each one of us there is a small, exciting and incalculable troll.

ISBN 0 948259 65 5   paper £8.95   160pp

SPRING TIDE

by Pia Tafdrup

Translated from the Danish by Anne Born

Spring Tide is a book about desire, about woman's passion. From inception through total immersion in sensual emotion towards an apprehension of winter's cold, Pia Tafdrup links personal ecstasy with the cyclic rhythm of life. Hailed by Scandinavian critics as a young Danish poet of exceptional talent, Pia Tafdrup, in this sustained sequence of thought-provoking poems, turns language into experience.

ISBN 0 948259 55 8   paper £6.95   96pp

ENCHANTING BEASTS

An anthology of modern women poets of Finland

Edited & Translated by Kirsti Simonsuuri

Marja-Liisa Vartio, Eeva-Liisa Manner, Mirkka Rekola, Sirkka Turkka, Satu Marttila, Eira Stenberg, Kirsti Simonsuuri, Tua Forsström, Arja Tiainen, Anne Hänninen, Annukka Peura – bringing the English-speaking reader some of the best modern poetry from Finland. Some of the poets have never been translated before, and some have already small volumes in translation, or poems in English anthologies to their credit. High lyrical intensity, brave honesty about the human condition, particularly about the female experience, wit, and a feeling for nature are characteristics shared by all of these poets writing in the northernmost corner of Europe, in a landscape of strong contrasts, of light and darkness.

ISBN 0 948259 68 X   144pp
£8.95 paper

MY BROTHER SEBASTIAN

by Annika Idström

Translated by Joan Tate

Annika Idström writes with a rare intensity and psychological insight. *My Brother Sebastian* is an unforgettable account of a lonely boy's exposure to the degradation of inhuman cruelty and the strong resistance of human intelligence in the struggle to survive.

ISBN 1 85610 002 2   144pp
£8.95